D1646242

WORDS OF WILLIAM BOOTH

£1·00

Words of William Booth

by
CYRIL BARNES

Salvationist Publishing and Supplies Ltd.,
Judd Street, King's Cross, London WC1H 9NN

ISBN 0 85412 269 9

LIEUT.-COLONEL CYRIL BARNES
became a Salvation Army officer in 1933. He served in corps work until 1948, since when he has been a member of the Literary Department at International Headquarters.

MADE AND PRINTED IN GREAT BRITAIN
IN 11PT. IMPRINT TYPE BY
THE CAMPFIELD PRESS, ST. ALBANS, HERTS.

Contents

Preface

THROUGHOUT the years the words of William Booth have been quoted to great purpose. Apart from his prolific writings and numerous addresses, many of his sayings were terse, sudden, used in repartee or in reprimand or warning. His hearers remembered them. They handed them down to succeeding generations. To place these brief expressions in their geographical and historical setting helps them to become filled with new life.

Each of the following short chapters, presented in as near a chronological order as possible, is a story in itself. Together they can serve as an introduction to the study of the life of a man of whom a Japanese newspaper in 1907 claimed: ' He speaks not as the professors, but as a man with a soul in possession of secrets.'

I loved my mother

ON April 10, 1829, in a terraced house which opened straight on to a Nottingham front garden, Mary Moss Booth gave birth to her third child, William, who, two days later, was to be christened in the church across the main road.

Mary Moss was the second wife of Samuel Booth, 15 years her senior. She was born in Somercotes, Derbyshire, in 1790, daughter of a farmer. Her mother died

William Booth's birthplace today

1

when Mary was three and the child had been brought up by a kind aunt and uncle and given a good religious training.

As a married woman, Mary found life to be anything but easy, but with natural wisdom and shrewdness she trained her son in the way he should go.

Although Mrs Booth knew poverty, whether as the wife of a speculative builder who was unable to meet his creditors, as a smallholder in Bleasby, or as a resident in ' a humble house ' in Sneinton Road, Nottingham, she kept a clean and respectable home for her son and his sisters.

When Samuel died, William was only 14 and, as his older brother had died in infancy, accepted responsibility for his mother. His income from his apprenticeship to a pawnbroker was low enough, but by 1849, when he moved to London, he had set her up in a small shop in Goose Gate where she sold needles, cotton and lace.

In the spring of 1855, while William was saving up to be married, and in the midst of a preaching campaign in the Potteries and the North of England, he visited Nottingham. When he left his mother he gave her five pounds, leaving himself only fifteen shillings and still greatly needing a new coat.

' *I loved my mother*,' he wrote in *All the World* (1893), ' yet one of the regrets which has followed me to the present hour is that I did not sufficiently value the treasure while I possessed it, and that I did not with sufficient tenderness and assiduity, at the time, attempt the impossible task of repaying the unmeasurable debt I owed that mother's love.'

William Booth wrote also of her efforts to remove misery, of never sending a beggar away empty-handed and of her commiseration with the sorrowing and unfortunate.

Mary died in 1875, while his work was still known as The Christian Mission with 19 stations and less than

2,000 members. Nevertheless, she had been one of her son's greatest admirers and prayerful supporters.

Periodically she would visit the Booth home in London. On one occasion she heard him preach on peace.

' William,' she said afterwards, ' you preached a beautiful sermon.'

' You've heard your son preach,' came the loving reply; ' how would you like to hear your son pray, just as he used to pray when he was a boy? '

Then the tall preacher became the son again and fell to his knees, and with face in his mother's lap prayed in simple terms for the love of God to be ever-increasingly his mother's portion.

Two

A new translation of the Bible

IMMEDIATELY after his conversion William Booth wondered ' what were all the novels . . . compared with the story of my Saviour? What were the choicest orators compared with Paul? ' From youth onward he became a student of the Book of books and could say, ' Thy word is a lamp unto my feet, and a light unto my path.'

When he preached his first sermon, he went to the cottage in Kid Street, Nottingham, well equipped. A member of the small congregation remembered the occasion well and described the scene nearly 70 years later: ' It was at eight o'clock at night. . . . There was a box placed upside down on the table for a desk, with two candles burning, one each side of the Bible.'

In London, as a Kennington pawnbroker's assistant, his resolutions of December 6, 1849, included the promise ' that I will read not less than four chapters in God's word every day '.

Three years later, when considering the call to the ministry, he met Dr John Campbell, the most influential among London Nonconformists. ' Now you must go to college and study the Bible,' he advised the prospective student, ' and what you find there you must go out and preach.'

Kid Street, Nottingham

Although William Booth did not enter the college, he carried out the rest of the advice implicitly. He became and remained a preacher of what he found in God's written word.

In 1885, as leader of an Army with 3,000 officers preaching in nearly one and a half million meetings a year, he felt it his duty to write in *The War Cry* about the Revised Version of the Bible. He considered its publication to be ' the event of the past week '.

The only complaint he made was that if he had had the arrangements he would have expressed its substance ' not in the stiff and ancient language used 300 years ago, but in the form of speech employed by the people of the present day '.

It would not be difficult to imagine his appreciation of some of the more recent translations, which have both retained the truth and been couched in language understood by those hitherto unfamiliar with the book which is still the world's bestseller.

Nevertheless, in his *War Cry* article he continued: ' If the Revision throws any new light upon the precious volume—the Book of books—I shall accept it very gratefully. Meanwhile . . . I want to see *a new translation of the Bible* into the hearts and conduct of living men and women. . . . It is no use making correct translations of words if we cannot get the words translated into life.'

Three

I don't mean to belong to the commonalty

WALTER JAMES, of Sneinton, otherwise unknown, was able to claim fame for having called from William Booth one of his most characteristic phrases.

The two young men were walking past the Nottingham church where, less than twenty years earlier, Samuel Booth had taken his two-day-old son William to be christened according to Anglican rites.

' Have you no ambition? ' Booth's boy suddenly asked his companion.

' What do you mean? ' came the surprised response.

' Because I have,' William continued; ' I intend to be something great; *I don't mean to belong to the commonalty.*'

Before long, Nottingham was not big enough to hold this man who meant to be something. The day would come when England would be too small. In those mid-1840s the Lord's words to Ananias, ' He is a chosen vessel unto Me, to bear My name before . . . Kings ', could have been used for William Booth with as much truth as for Paul.

At that time there seemed little prospect of fulfilment for the precariously placed pawnbroker's apprentice, but about 60 years later, by 1907, it had become the order of the day.

In January of that year the Army General's journal, written in Copenhagen, contained the note: ' Interview with the King and Queen in the afternoon. . . . Most friendly. . . . Lasted . . . an hour and a quarter.'

A few days later, in Christiania (Oslo), he wrote: ' Interview with the King 12 noon '; and before the week was out he was in Stockholm, where he enjoyed conversation with the Queen, the King being ' too ill to see anyone'.

Before the summer came the one-time Sneinton boy was as far from home as he could be, in the Japanese Emperor's palace listening to the musical voice of His Imperial Majesty.

In a letter to his grandchildren William Booth described the thrill of the occasion: ' So unusual is it for any but princes of kingly blood or the direct representatives of friendly governments to be admitted into the royal presence.' He heard the Emperor express his sympathy with the good work of William Booth's followers.

A month later the Army's General was receiving an honorary doctorate at Oxford University.

Monarchs and presidents recognized that he did not ' belong to the commonalty '; leaders of education showed their appreciation; he counted among his friends princes of the Church; those attending his funeral service in Olympia included Britain's Queen Mary; and on the Army's Centenary Day (1965), Commissioner Wycliffe Booth unveiled a memorial to his grandfather in Westminster Abbey.

Nevertheless, William Booth knew that worldly success was of little value compared with the importance of hearing his Heavenly Master's ' well done '.

Four

Nobody wants me!

' THERE is no way for me. *Nobody wants me!*' exclaimed William Booth in April 1852 in conversation with Edward Harris Rabbits, the 31-year-old Walworth bootmaker.

Three years earlier the Army's Founder had been forced because of unemployment to leave his home town and take up work in a pawnbroker's shop in Kennington, London. He had grown to hate the trade. He felt out of it in business life. His ticket of membership had not been renewed with one branch of the Methodist Church. He had changed his allegiance to another.

He had heard the call to be a full-time preacher, but nobody gave him any hope of seeing his longings fulfilled. Even his application to be a chaplain on a convict ship bound for Australia had been rejected. He felt he was out, out with everyone.

Then Mr Rabbits made an offer. He assured William that the Methodist group with whom he had recently allied himself wanted an evangelist and, what is more, Mr. Rabbits would support him financially for at least the first three months.

William's immediate reaction revealed his despondency, a gloom which was soon dispelled as he saw in his benefactor's suggestion the over-ruling hand of God.

As the years passed he who was wanted by no one became sought after the world over.

Fifty-three years later, when the City of London wanted to bestow its Freedom on this prince of evangelists and social pioneers, he was invited to the Guildhall, the city's civic palace.

He for whom a splendid coach would have been provided chose to make the journey from his headquarters in Queen Victoria Street on foot. Had he not walked through those same streets in late June 1865 on his way to Mile End Waste and the Blind Beggar?

The City Chamberlain, Sir Joseph Dimsdale, in presenting the casket referred to the General's labours for

The City Chamberlain presenting the casket

mankind, then continued: 'These monuments of work well done will outlive decay's effacing fingers.'

The casket itself, instead of being made of some expensive metal was, by the General's desire, of wood carved out of an oaken beam once in the structure of the Guildhall. A donation of £100 to assist his work among the needy completed the value of the gift.

In his reply the General's mind was on those whom nobody wanted. 'The Army', he claimed, 'has invited the drunkard, the harlot, the criminal, the pauper, the friendless . . . to come and seek God. It has gone to those classes who are not found in the churches, who are without hope and help.'

Another seven decades have passed and that still is and *must be* the Army's mission. To quote the document on which the name 'Salvation Army' was first written, converts must be 'recruited from amongst the multitudes who are without God and without hope '.

Five

I want to make a sermon

FROM among the collections of courtship correspondence preserved for curious eyes to see, the love-letters which passed between William and Catherine Booth must be almost unique.

William's included descriptions of his health and his diet, an assessment of his congregations, his opinions of international affairs, and his longing for the days when they would be together. Here and there the usual order would be broken by short, clear declarations of his love for ' my own dear Kate '.

After writing in his typical manner from an evangelistic campaign in Staffordshire, he added a postscript: ' *I want to make a sermon* on the Flood; if anything strikes you on the subject, note it down.'

The subject must have concerned him, for he repeated the request on another occasion, and added the subjects of Jonah and of the Judgment. He wanted bare thoughts, ' some clear outlines '. He had confidence in Catherine's knowledge of divine truth and of the needs of men. He continued, ' We must have that kind of truth which will move sinners.'

Whenever William Booth opened the Bible to speak, he preached for decisions. He deplored the fact that when he spoke too calmly few people came forward to pray.

He repeated a subject—if he felt it contained the right message for the occasion and crowd.

One sermon for which he was remembered in many lands was about the treachery of Judas. 'Ah!' he would ask suddenly, ' who is this? See his sunken eyes, his hollow cheeks, his tottering gait, his bent form, his streaming eyes, his out-stretched hands. What is the man doing? '

Then he would start counting—' 1, 2, 3 . . . '. The congregation would become more and more electrified as he reached ' 28, 29, 30! '

' That ', he would then shout, ' is Judas, the prince of backsliders. And if ever you go to hell, he will come to you and count his silver in your ears, and you will show him the price paid for your soul, too.'

But that was not the end of his sermon—he spoke of the love of God and the price Christ paid for man's redemption.

When Bramwell, his son, summed up the old prophet's preaching substance, he wrote: ' He did not stand before the up-turned faces of thousands in order to spin out a philosophical theology. His great appeal was to the conscience. He believed that in every individual there was a judgment seat . . . reminding men also of that solemn bar of God.'

William Booth in the early 1860s

This was written long after William had died, but could

have been truthfully stated as early as 1877 when his preaching ' hit the headlines ' in Leicester.

At eight o'clock on the morning of July 31, 26-year-old John Starkey was hanged at the local jail for murdering his wife. Twelve hours later William Booth preached ' Starkey's funeral sermon ' to a crowd of 2,000 in ' the salvation warehouse ', using the text, ' Except ye repent . . .'. In the prayer meeting which followed, ' the Penitent-form was soon filled with anxious souls '.

Six

My dear wife wishes to speak

IT was Whit-Sunday 1860 and the congregation filling Bethesda Chapel, Gateshead, had been listening to William Booth preaching. The testimonies also had been powerful and Catherine Booth ' felt the Holy Spirit come upon me . . . to the extremities of my hands and feet '.

No longer could she sit still and listen. If necessary she would be ' a fool for Christ '. She must publicly testify to her faith.

Leaving the minister's pew and holding four-year-old Bramwell's hand she walked up the aisle toward the pulpit. Already she had four children and Emma Moss was only four months old. William thought something had happened to his wife. The congregation joined in the concern for they all knew Catherine's timid nature.

William left the pulpit to inquire if all was well. When he received his wife's explanation that she wanted ' to say a word ' he was so surprised that he was able to do no more than announce, ' *My dear wife wishes to speak*', and sit down.

Up till then Catherine had worked behind the scenes. She had visited the people in their homes and invited

Bethesda Chapel, Gateshead

them to the services. She had led in prayer. A few months before, she had written a 32-page pamphlet, still read today, on *Female Ministry*. On Whit-Sunday morning she put her theories into practice.

News of Mrs Booth's ' break through ' reached home before she did.

' The mistress has spoken! ' shouted the servant, who had been in the service. She danced round the kitchen.

That evening Catherine preached in William's place! And from that day on seldom was there a Sunday—when health permitted, and often when it did not—when she was not preaching the gospel.

William Booth's announcement from the Gateshead pulpit was given at a time when women preachers were almost unknown, but he accepted Catherine's action as a sign from God. His words remain a challenge to women everywhere.

From the earliest days of The Christian Mission he gave women equal places with men. His rules, formulated in 1870, contained a clause stating that women ' shall be employed as preachers itinerant or otherwise and class leaders and as such shall have appointments given to them on the preachers' plan; and they shall be eligible for any office, and to speak and vote at all official meetings '.

Little wonder, then, that women have been the pioneers of Army work in Wales (1874), Ireland (1880), France (1881) and Sweden (1882), and members of the pioneer parties sent to almost all other new openings.

Seven

I have found my destiny!

To find a man dead in the gutter was a common sight. Starvation was the verdict. To find working men of London's East End darkening church doors was the unusual.

Into a setting like this walked William Booth, a six-foot-one Methodist minister without a church, on a sultry June evening in 1865. Throughout England and Wales he had won hundreds of people for God; but he was unsettled, his future was undecided.

He stopped when he reached the pavement outside ' The Blind Beggar '. A group of men holding an open-air meeting attracted his attention. When they finished speaking they asked him to ' have a word '.

A few days later, representatives of that group begged him to take charge of a mission they were conducting in a tent on a disused Quaker burial ground between Vallance

Road and Fulbourne Street, Whitechapel. Their leader had fallen sick; would he help them out?

Consequently, on Sunday evening (July 2) he preached the gospel to between two and three hundred people in an unventilated tent illuminated by evil-smelling naphtha lamps.

The Whitechapel tent

What a beginning! But in that meeting six people 'came forward' and from it grew the world-wide work of The Salvation Army.

After one of these weekly meetings William Booth reached his home at 31 Shaftesbury (now Ravenscourt) Road, Hammersmith, about midnight, tired but strangely excited. He who had earlier said, 'I would be a missionary for God', had found his mission field. To his wife, Catherine, awaiting her beloved's arrival, he exclaimed: '*I have found my destiny!*'

Catherine was with him in his determination. She became his greatest supporter, his valued adviser. Together, they built The Salvation Army. July 2 is rightly called Founders' Day—implying that the work was not of one only, but of both.

Eight

These are our people

LATE one Sunday night, William Booth was returning home. He had had a busy day preaching the gospel. Twelve-year-old Bramwell was with him.

They had left Mile End Waste and gone but a few yards along Cambridge Heath Road when William pushed open the door of a drinking saloon. What Bramwell saw he never forgot. As a grown man he recalled seeing a ' brilliantly lighted place, noxious with the fumes of drink and tobacco, and reeking of filth. . . . The place was crowded with men, many of them bearing on their faces the marks of brutishness and vice, and with women also, dishevelled and drunken.'

As the lad looked wondering what was the cause of all this sorrow, his father said: ' *Willie, these are our people; these are the people I want you to live for and bring to Christ*.'

' These people '—who could find company in their loneliness and drown their sorrows by getting drunk—had nothing but the public house. There, according to Hogarth's engraving ' Gin Lane ' in the British Museum, they could be ' drunk for a penny and dead drunk for tuppence '. If too drunk to go home, the unfortunate victim of gin could be given ' clean straw for nothing '. ' Oh, Kate,' William had already declared to his wife, Catherine, ' where can you go and find such heathen as these, and where is there so great a need for your labours? '

Early indoor congregations were made up of such people. ' No one in the audience seemed worth sixpence,' described an observer of the meeting in the Dancing Academy, New Road, Whitechapel, in the autumn of 1865. Worth sixpence, of course, in giving power; to the Army's Founder every one was a ' precious soul '.

A few months later, a crowd gathered to hear him preach in the Effingham Theatre evoked from a reporter the remark that ' the boxes and stalls were filled with as idle and dissolute a set of characters as ever crossed a place of public worship '; and another referred to their ' pale and careworn features '.

' Our people ' are still the lonely and needy, but today we find them in over 80 countries.

Nine

Never a Christmas Day like this again!

THE Booth family had moved to a new house and they were determined to have the happiest Christmas Day yet. Father would be out preaching in the morning: after that he would have fun and games with the children—all eight of them, from 12-year-old Bramwell to Lucy seeing her first Christmas.

The children eagerly awaited his home-coming, but the father who returned to 3 Gore Road, Hackney, appeared to be a different man from the one who had left earlier. ' He looked dreadfully white and drawn, just as if he were ill or harassed by some grievous worry,' recalled a friend living with the family.

' *I'll never have a Christmas Day like this again!* ' he cried in a state of great agitation. He had seen Christmas from a new angle as he passed along the Whitechapel streets. He was heartbroken. ' The poor have nothing

The Booths' home in Gore Road

but the public-house — nothing but the public-house! '
That was the last Christmas Day he spent at home.

The next 12 months was a period of advancement.
Work was commenced for the first time outside the
Borough of Tower Hamlets, at Croydon.   By April
breakfasts were being served to nearly 900 hungry poor
in the East London (Effingham) Theatre.

Preparations for the next Christmas (1869) were put in
hand soon after the ' sad day ' in Gore Road.

A small sheet was printed and distributed far and wide.

It read: ' We are arranging to give 4 lbs of beef, a plum pudding and 1 oz of tea to each of 300 families on Christmas Day, and we hope to be able to do much more.'

The same sheet contained a place where donations could be recorded under the heading: ' Offerings made at the breakfast table on Christmas Day 1869 for the destitute members of the household of faith and the sick and starving poor of the East of London.' The appeal raised about £100.

When the day arrived those of the Booth household who were old enough were out among the needy distributing cheer, which included puddings made in the kitchen at Gore Road. Three hundred people received a Christmas dinner, ' most of whom would have dined on a cup of tea and a bit of dry bread '.

William Booth appreciated the Christmas spirit. He was soon writing: ' It is considered the correct thing to wish everybody a merry Christmas, and to get one yourself if you can. . . . We like the word " merry ", and we will have it in our religion if you please. . . . We should be hypocrites if we were not merry. . . . There's a time for everything, and this is the merry time.'

When wishing his *War Cry* readers of 1884 ' a merry Christmas ', William Booth reminded them that ' true salvation merriment is possible only where the soul is discharging its duty to man '.

Ten

Look after the children!

DR THOMAS BARNARDO, guardian of orphaned children, and William Booth met in Limehouse, in a building which had been a low-grade penny gaff—it had recently been converted into a Christian Mission hall.

The doctor—at that time still a student at the London Hospital—and the preacher worked together until they saw they each had a special calling to fulfil. ' You look after the children and I'll look after the adults,' said the missioner as he bade the medico farewell. ' Then together we'll convert the world.'

William Booth's work among children had been disappointing. He had held young lads' prayer meetings as early as September 1865, and was running small ' Sabbath schools ' by 1866, but the initial progress had not been maintained.

In his opening address to the 1877 Conference, after dealing with the work and plans of the Mission, he suddenly turned to the needs of young people. ' We have not as yet any real plan to propose for dealing with the children,' he declared. ' It must be distinctly understood that no new school must be commenced; in fact, no new plan of any kind must be adopted anywhere without my consent.'

When, in July 1880, Captain John Roberts started his meetings for boys and girls in Blyth, Northumberland, that rule was still in operation. Nevertheless, when General Booth saw that one of his officers was on to a good thing, he changed his views and ordered similar work to be inaugurated in all corps.

By December 6, 1884, he was writing in *The War Cry*: ' God speed the rising race. . . . Get them saved. . . . Possess their minds with truth. . . . Teach them your music, and hurry them on in every possible way to get ready for the fight.'

During his 1905 motor tour of England and Scotland he stopped in the Market Square at Buckingham. He spoke of people he wanted to see won for God. Then he suddenly turned to a group of smiling children standing on a farm-cart platform and exclaimed: ' In God's name let us work as we never worked before for the little ones of the world! '

A young people's march in 1888

When blind and dying, the old warrior still loved the 'rising race' and appealed to his eldest son: 'Ah, my boy, we don't know what it means to be without a home. . . . The homeless children. *Oh, the children! Bramwell, look after the children!* Promise me.'

Eleven

On the side of law and order

THE CHRISTIAN MISSION was less than four years old when the first clash occurred with the police. Brothers Rose and Fisher, who were connected with the mission station in Three Colts Lane, Bethnal Green (' the wool shed '), were holding an open-air meeting.

They were arrested when they would not desist and on the way to the station sang, 'Jesus, the name high over all '. On arrival they gave tracts to the policemen on duty and prayed aloud.

A fortnight later they stood before the magistrate to answer a summons brought against them by a local publican, in whose opinion the missioners had ' disturbed the quiet of his customers, would not let his children sleep, nor him and his wife read '.

Fortunately, the magistrate found no cause for a conviction and, being ' bound over in their own recognisances not to repeat the same offence in that particular locality for six months ', the accused went on their way rejoicing.

William Booth regretted this collision with authority and to the report added his own thoughts. ' We are *on the side of law and order*,' he wrote, ' and wish to work harmoniously with those who are paid guardians of the same.'

As the years passed and his work grew, as drunkards became respectable citizens, as wife-beaters became home-builders, as the wayward became upright, so enemies multiplied. They found ridiculous by-laws which made the work of William Booth and his followers appear to be illegal. They overlooked the purpose and spirit and breathed vengeance.

Again, in 1886, the Army's Founder wrote: ' Our earnest desire is to live peaceably with all men.' ' But', he went on, ' they can fine us, imprison us, do what they like with us, but shall we never go back? Never! '

During following years, until offending laws were changed and public attitudes amended, hundreds of Salvationists in many lands went to prison or were assaulted in the streets.

At Wigston a 10-day convert was sent to prison ' to be reformed from expressing the joy of the newly found salvation louder than the devil likes '. At Stockton the Captain played a cornet, at Truro a concertina, at Buckingham a drum; the girl-Captain at York sang a solo—and all went to prison for their ' crime '.

In 1884 the Salvationist population in British prisons during the year numbered 600—and almost every land has its own stories of persecution and misunderstanding.

William Booth's words have long since been seen as truth, and in Stockport an intended additional police station was never built because Salvationist influence did away with the need.

Twelve

Cold feet and toothache

WILLIAM BOOTH needed £3,000. At least that was the price of the building he had seen which would accommodate the crowds attending his meetings in Whitechapel.

His Mission was three years old and the forgotten of the East End of London felt they had a champion. The proposed building, a People's Market which had failed, contained a large hall for meetings, 10 smaller rooms, a shop at the front and a soup kitchen complete with steam engine and copper. The place would be an ' untold boon to the starving poor, who came from miles around '.

The first announcement of this project included the statement that ' the poor people themselves have been contributing for some time toward a place and have stored up something like £300 '.

A general appeal brought immediate response, donations varying from an anonymous gift of £250 to a shilling. A butcher, converted earlier in the year, promised: ' The

Lord has blessed me greatly. I am feeding eight pigs for Christmas and I shall give Him four of them for the People's Market.'

The People's Mission Hall

Gifts also began to pour in for a public sale and among

the first was a sewing machine, a diamond and ruby ring—valued at £50, and a large solitaire scarf pin.

Money came in fast but the negotiations were slow. However, after 12 months, the price had been reduced to £1,750—a great help when almost £1,000 more would be needed for alterations.

When considering these changes one committee member suggested that, instead of leaving the stone paving, the floor should be asphalted.

' No! ' cried William Booth, ' poor people feel the cold quite as much, if not more, than do rich people. We shall have a wooden floor and the place shall be heated by hot water apparatus. *No one gets a blessing if they have cold feet and nobody ever got saved while they had toothache!* '

William Booth had his way and the People's Mission Hall was opened on his next birthday, April 10, 1870.

Today the Army has outgrown the building, but the Founder's words are still true. Who listens to sermons when he is perishing with cold? Who can think of anything else when suffering pain?

When a man's bodily needs have received attention he is more likely to listen to the story of the love of God which has inspired the friend who has offered the helping hand.

Thirteen

All the year round

IT is often said—and truly—that the Army began in the open air. It was while standing with a group of missioners in a meeting on the pavement outside ' The Blind Beggar ' in London's East End that the Army's Founder saw the real need of the unchurched crowds. The official birth of the Army was a few days later in a tent, but open-air meetings always preceded indoor gatherings and were a means of attracting a congregation.

One of William Booth's first books was entitled *How to Reach the Masses with the Gospel*. The reading of it drew George Scott Railton, later Secretary of The Christian Mission and the Army's first Commissioner, to his side. It contained many records of open-air successes.

Christian Missioners believed, as Salvationists still do, that if people would not, or could not, come to them, they would go to the people.

William Booth believed that God had given him ' a mission to the throngs in the great thoroughfares teeming about on the Sabbath Day, and all other days '. He wrote about the need for spreading the gospel not only during the summer but throughout the dark dreary evenings of the winter. He then went on: ' *Hence we continue our open-air work all the year round.*'

In some countries open-air meetings are allowed only with special permission, but elsewhere Salvationists have free use of the streets—a privilege won at great cost.

William Booth's followers always find a way of reaching the masses.

How interested a group of English holiday-makers to Switzerland were to read a notice in German, nailed to a telephone post, inviting them to an open-air meeting! Those who accepted would hear Army music, singing and speaking at 14.30 hours on Sunday; but the Salvationists would be at Oschinsee, 2,000 feet higher up the mountains, for that was where the crowds would be.

Today, in many lands, the Army open-air meeting has become part of national life. How often when television producers want to set the scene for a Sunday morning they have a group of Army people on the street!

The open-air meeting is the place where many Salvationists first learn to speak in public, and an old Army chorus states the timeless truth: 'There's something in the open air that makes you want to do and dare.'

Fourteen

Burn those sermons

IN the early days of the Army, William Booth was conducting a meeting in Whitechapel with a congregation of 1,200 people. Normally his speaking was dynamic; he could hold a crowd spellbound. But on this particular night the number of godless people was higher than usual; some were quite violent and he was making no impression.

Among his supporters was a gipsy hawker who had been converted a few weeks earlier. He was called to the platform to tell of the change in his life.

As soon as he began to speak silence reigned. He was well known, not as a preacher but for his wayward living. His words were bungling—but they rang true. The attention of the crowd was recaptured.

'Willie,' said the Founder to Bramwell when the meeting was over, '*I shall have to burn all those old sermons of mine, and go in for the gipsy's.*'

William Booth's sermons had been the means of leading many people into a knowledge of God's salvation, but if the testimony method was more powerful, then testimony had to be given a greater place in his meetings. With this occasion in mind, he later wrote that ' ordinary working-men in their corduroys and bowler hats could command attention from their own class which was refused point-blank to me with my theological terms and superior knowledge '.

When the Edinburgh Castle preaching station was opened in Stepney, Mrs Eliza Collingridge, a Christian Mission bible-woman, was there. Little is known about the ceremony beyond the fact that she gave her testimony. God used her words and John Gore was converted. Thirteen years later, with Edward Saunders, he started Army work in Australia.

Richard Slater, the 'father of Salvation Army music', was won for God after hearing the faltering testimony of a servant girl.

Richard Slater

William Booth never debunked preaching: he believed in giving everything its right time and place. In 1890, he wrote: 'What is the use of preaching the gospel to men whose whole attention is concentrated upon a mad, desperate struggle to keep themselves alive? . . . The first thing to do is to get him at least a footing on firm ground, and give him room to live. Then . . . you will have a better opportunity to find a way to his heart, if he comes to know that it was you who pulled him out of the horrible pit and the miry clay in which he was sinking to perdition.'

Fifteen

A Penitent-form man?

ILLNESS had befallen William Booth. He had already been away from home for three months and was staying with friends at Tunbridge Wells. He was suffering from a nervous breakdown caused by overwork.

Although fears had been expressed that he might not be able to take up his leadership of The Christian Mission again, he was feeling ' much better the last day or two ' and his mind was beginning to fill with future plans.

It was June 18, 1872, when he claimed this improvement in health in a letter to William Stephenson Crow.

Mr Crow was a Gateshead printer. He was the first to use in print the term ' Hallelujah Lasses ' for women preachers. He attended the War Congress of 1878 as a representative of the ' unoccupied north '. Later he moved to London and became the printer of the first 12 editions of *The War Cry*.

But with William Booth he held a special connection: he was the Mission leader's confidant.

A new evangelist was being considered and Mr Crow was asked: ' Now about D—. Let him write me. My secretary will send you a list of questions for him to answer. Would he understand or be able to learn anything of missioning the streets? If he is such a man as I conceive from your letter we could find him work. . . . Is D—a revivalist? *A Penitent-form man?* That is the main thing.'

Already William Booth had spoken clearly on this subject. On Easter Monday (1871) in the People's Mission Hall, in Whitechapel, he declared: ' Our cry is still, " Souls, souls, souls! " We are still a Penitent-form people; we believe in getting sinners to the Penitent-form.'

Every Salvation Army hall still has its Penitent-form;

it is the focal point of all Salvationist endeavour. Yet it is not so much a place as an idea.

As a boy, in 1844, William Booth knelt on the floor in the middle of a downstairs room of the Wesley Chapel, Broad Street, Nottingham. That spot became his Penitent-form because there he confessed his sins, met with God, received His forgiveness and became converted.

Sixteen

I am a bit of a 'comic' myself

IN May 1873 William Booth visited Portsmouth to conduct a service in a music hall which the missioners rented until they leased a more permanent building in Lake Road. As he approached the door, he stopped to greet a man who was obviously interested in the crowd going into the building.

'Are you a Christian?' he inquired.

'A Christian?' the man challenged. 'Do you know who I am? I am the " comic " in this music hall! '

' Well,' replied the visitor, ' *I am a bit of a " comic " myself.*'

William Booth recalled the incident during his sermon and his humour was not lost on the congregation. 'Are there not some things more tragical than comical?' he continued; and made a lasting impression on at least one lad—John Roberts, who became the pioneer of children's work in the Army and the first editor of *The Little Soldier* (later *The Young Soldier*).

Although as a youth William was extremely serious and possessed ' nothing of that humorous spirit which characterized so much of his later work ', his comicality helped him in many a situation and often roused his listeners from their lethargy.

Peter Monk, once a prize-fighter and one of the earliest Mission converts in the Whitechapel Tent, in describing his leader's addresses said: ' It seemed as if he'd tear the soul out of your body. And then in the midst of it all there'd be a bit that would make you want to cry, or a tale that would set you laughing fit to burst! '

His lectures were not devoid of humour. He would tell of the Army's beginnings and development, then swing a quick change. He would tell of the ostler forced into conversation by an insistent Salvationist, who, as he was about to mount again, recited: ' Matthew, Mark, Luke and John, hold this horse while I get on.'

As soon as the laughing began to die out, the General would make a heart-rending appeal for sympathy and support.

In the 1880s, he would be indignant on hearing of the persecution and suffering of his followers, then joyfully exclaim: ' They only help to advertise us.'

When speaking to his officers he knew how to sweeten the medicine. On one occasion he wanted to tell them how to win the roughs for Christ. ' How not to reach them ', was the subject he announced. One point he made was—' Don't let them come where you are, if you can help it. Have door-keepers who will keep them out of your halls, or throw them down the stairs if they do come in, because they don't behave like ladies and gentlemen.'

Even when he was dying, humour did not leave him. Looking at his son and thinking of the problems facing a new General, he warned: ' I'm leaving you a bonnie handful! '

Seventeen

Three devils

ADDRESSING the Christian Mission Conference in June 1877, William Booth spoke on the value of good singing. There were less than 30 stations at this time, but in some places there seems to have been an attempt to make the singing too stiff, too professional. The standard must remain as it had been in the Effingham Theatre in 1867 when a visitor reported: ' " There is a better world, they say " was sung with such intensity and vigour.'

The Mission's repertoire consisted of hymns and gospel songs from the churches. The first Army song, ' Come, join our Army, to battle we go ', was yet to be written— that was to come during the next year, 1878.

The singing must be hearty and congregational. The order was: ' Sing hymns with salvation in them.' Solos should be given a place, both indoors and in the streets, but choirs the Founder would not tolerate.

' I have ever found choirs to be possessed of three devils, awkward, ugly—the quarrelling devil, the dressing devil, and the courting devil. We don't want to have choirs. Should you ever find a choir in connection with any hall in this mission, I give you my authority to take a besom and sweep it out, promising that you do it as lovingly as possible.'

Years later, when bands had become an accepted part of Army organization, William Booth saw the value of group music. He realized the help that could be given by people trained to sing—as long as it came from those ' whose hearts are full of the Spirit of God '.

In 1892 he allowed *The War Cry* to ask the question: ' Should not The Salvation Army have well-trained choirs as well as bands? '

The Salvationists of Kilmarnock I (Temple) lost no

time in giving a practical answer and formed its own singing brigade. Six years later, in September 1898, the London corps of Penge introduced its own commissioned songster brigade of 24 people.

By 1914, 13,000 had followed the Penge Salvationists' example, a number which has become five times larger during the past 60 years.

William Booth would have been the first to acknowledge the value of their service in helping to build up the Kingdom of God.

Eighteen

Children on both sides

EASTERN Europe had been in turmoil. War between Russia and Turkey had ended; a treaty had been signed, but the outcome was questionable. Further war, involving more countries, seemed highly probable.

William Booth, ever up to date in applying Christian principles to world events, wrote in *The Christian Mission Magazine* for May 1878: ' Let every one who values the favour of God do what in them lies to prevent such war.'

As General he remained a man of peace. When war raised its ugly head in South Africa in 1899 he was more than ever alarmed. He was involved and, in his diary, uttered a heart-broken cry: ' I am like a father with a divided household. *My children are on both sides.* Whoever wins, I lose.'

Later, throughout two world wars, those children of his remained brothers and sisters.

One night in a camp for British prisoners-of-war during the early 1940s, a German medical attendant went to bed.

First Salvation Army hut on a field of battle,
South Africa

He was tired, and delayed taking particulars of his most recent patient until the morning.

Dozing into sleep, the orderly, in civilian life a Salvation Army Bandmaster from Hamburg, heard an Army tune being whistled from the other side of his blanket partition.

When the music stopped, he continued with the chorus; and the impromptu programme went on for a while—until the Bandmaster could bear the suspense no longer. He pulled back the blanket, to find his latest admission with tears in his eyes but a smile on his face. The orderly, now Lieut.-Colonel Walter Flade, and the patient, now Auxiliary-Captain Charles Williams, shared true Christian fellowship.

During that same period of international upheaval, young people met for councils in a small hall belonging to the Berlin Temple Corps. Among those attending were workers conscripted from other lands. Dutch bandsmen played by the side of Germans; young Salvationists from France added strength to the singing; and a Swiss officer led the gatherings.

The Army Founder's longing for world peace was echoed by the then Chief of the Staff (Commissioner Arnold Brown) as he addressed the Rotary International Convention in Lausanne in May 1973: ' Peace begins in the individual spirit. Thereafter its concentric rings widen to include those in the home and family, the neighbours across the road or across an ocean. . . . World peace begins when we succeed in bringing the spirit of peace to one man, or woman, who is without it.'

Nineteen

We are sent to war

' *We are sent to war*,' cried William Booth as he opened his address at the War Congress in July 1878. ' We are not sent to minister to a congregation and be content if we keep things going. We are sent to make war . . . and to stop short of nothing but the subjugation of the world to the sway of the Lord Jesus.'

Two days before, the Congress had been opened with the singing of ' Sound the battle-cry. See the foe is nigh '. The next day, during the afternoon session under the title of ' War Memories ', Elijah Cadman had told of his arrival in Whitby nine months earlier.

The people had thought he was a madman for he had written out a bill proclaiming ' war on Whitby ' and had called for 2,000 men and women to join his ' Hallelujah Army '. He had signed the bill ' Captain Cadman '. ' So that's how I got my title,' he told his fellow evangelists, soon to adopt the title themselves.

By the time of the War Congress the change of name from ' The Christian Mission ' to ' The Salvation Army ' was being accepted. Over the platform of the Whitechapel hall, where the main meetings were being held, hung a sign bearing the painted letters ' Salvation Army '. It had been placed there, on the instruction of Bramwell Booth, by William H. Ebdon, who, a few months later, designed the Army crest.

Already, in May of that year, the greatest force in the ' war ' idea had been felt by the stroke of a pen. Bramwell Booth and George Scott Railton had begun work early in the office of the Booth household. They had received the proofs of the 1878 report of the work of the Mission and were reading them when William Booth, still in his dressing gown, walked into the room.

The report stated that ' The Christian Mission . . . is a Volunteer Army recruited from amongst the multitudes who are without God and without hope in the world,

. . . and wrote, ' Salvation '

devoting their leisure time to all sorts of laborious efforts for the salvation of others '.

Looking over Railton's shoulder, the General Superintendent (William Booth) was fired with inspiration.

' No! ' he exclaimed with unmistakable certainty; ' we are not volunteers, for we feel we *must* do what we do, and we are always on duty.' Pen in hand, he crossed out ' Volunteer ' and wrote ' Salvation '.

A century later Salvationists still sign *Articles of War* on becoming *soldiers*. They pay their weekly envelope offering in the form of a *cartridge*; the giving of which is called ' firing '. Converts are *prisoners*; and early-morning prayer meeting is a *knee-drill*. In all their Christian service Salvationists follow Paul's injunction to ' put on the whole armour of God '.

Twenty

Decided on the flag

WILLIAM BOOTH was in the middle of an eight-week tour of the midlands and north of England. On Monday, October 7, 1878, he wrote from Barnsley to Captain Elijah Cadman, in charge of the two-year-old corps in Leeds.

' I am on my way north,' the letter read. ' Shall be at Sheffield tonight, Mexborough tomorrow . . . Bradford Friday till Monday, when I propose to come to Leeds. Mrs Booth is with me. *We have at length decided on the flag* and Mrs Booth is presenting the colours to each corps as we go along and she will do so to your troops on Monday night as well.'

Already, during the week-end of September 28 to 30, the Salvationists at Coventry had rejoiced in being the recipients of the first of all Army flags, and that also from the hands of Catherine Booth.

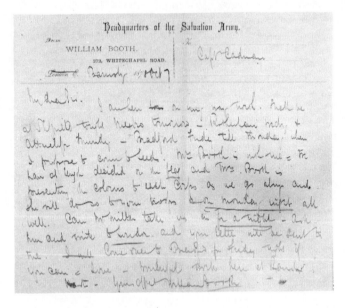

The idea of a flag had been in the minds of the Army's Founders for some years—even in the days of The Christian Mission. In May 1876 William Booth wrote to Mrs Billups, financial supporter and trusted friend: ' We are thinking of getting a flag, and if so, of crimson ground and blue border. What do you think?—the crimson signifying the atonement and the blue, purity.'

In *These Fifty Years* Bramwell Booth attributed the inception of the flag to his mother: ' While the Founder had the creative genius, she had the analytical mind. He made things, she improved them. He inspired the Army, raised its colours (though literally the Army flag was her idea, and the design finally resolved upon was hers).'

When presenting colours, in May 1879, to the corps at Newcastle upon Tyne, Catherine said: ' The crimson represents the precious Blood by which we were all redeemed; the blue is God's chosen emblem of purity; the sun represents both light and heat, the light and life of men; and the motto, " Blood and Fire ", the Blood of the Lamb, and the fire of the Holy Spirit ' (*The Salvationist*, June 1879). When pioneers went to India, in 1882, the sun was changed to a star to avoid causing offence to the Parsees, to whom the sun is a sacred symbol.

On July 2, 1965, the Army flag was to be seen fluttering in the gentle breeze over the tower of Westminster Abbey while inside thousands of people sang praises to God for 100 years of divine guidance and protection.

Twenty-one

Pens dipped in the love of God

' SURE, General, if you think it will do any good,' replied a wag, a New York pressman, after William Booth had asked if he might pray with him and a group of his colleagues at the end of an interview.

' O Lord,' the General prayed, ' bless these boys here. They have been useful to Thy servant. Save some of them. Thou knowest we are in need of some smart consecrated up-to-date men with *pens dipped in the love of God*. . . . Bless the editors of the papers that they represent. May they be fair and daring directors of their gift.'

On another occasion, when arriving in New Zealand by mail steamer, he was greeted by a group of prominent journalists who quickly found the Army leader to be ' good copy '.

When they had talked themselves dry William Booth inquired smilingly: 'Answered all your questions, gentlemen? '

After being assured that it had been a good interview, he let them know he had been glad to oblige, then continued: ' Now, having given you nearly half an hour of my time, I'll ask you for a few minutes of yours.' Whereupon he knelt down on the deck and invited them to join him in prayer.

William Booth always believed in the power of the printed word and in the inestimable value of writers whose pens are dipped in the love of God.

After publishing his own penny monthly magazine for 11 years he issued his first weekly *War Cry* on December 27, 1879. Printed in Fieldgate Street, Whitechapel, by William Crow and supervised in the final stages by Bramwell Booth, 17,000 copies were ready the night before for despatch throughout the country.

The problems created by an old constantly-breaking-down printing machine were surpassed only by the fact that a thick fog descended on Britain's capital; but thanks to Harry Tucker, who persuaded a stranded cab-driver to venture through the streets, all papers reached the stations in time to catch the trains.

Little did Harry know that 60 years later his nephew, Colonel Samuel Tucker, would be the Director of the Army's own Campfield Press.

To print and publish a paper is one thing; to get it into the hands of readers is another.

In the first edition of *Orders and Regulations for Field Officers* William Booth wrote: ' The circulation of *The War Cry* should be regarded by the field officer as a most important method of extending the Kingdom of God, and saving the souls of men.' And in a chapter entitled ' Fighting ' in the first edition of *Orders and Regulations for Salvation Soldiers* he urged that ' every soldier should make it a solemn duty to circulate every week either a small or large quantity of the paper '.

Twenty-two

Get your photographs taken

THE Sheffield Blades, a thousand-strong mob of ruffians, hated The Salvation Army. News that William and Catherine Booth were to lead a procession through their streets inspired them to make an attack which would drive all Salvationists beyond the city boundaries once and for all.

On January 16, 1882, the Army's procession organized by Major Elijah Cadman, got under way. It included a brass band mounted on a wagonette, Lieutenant Emmerson Davison on a white horse, and a carriage bearing General and Mrs Booth. Uniformed soldiers followed in orderly ranks.

The cloth-capped Blades lined the pavements, armed with a variety of missiles. Few police were there to curb their intentions.

The Sheffield riots

Suddenly the shrieking ruffians spilled across the road-way and hurled mud, sharp stones, sticks and rotten vegetables in well-aimed volleys.

The equestrian Lieutenant was the main target. A stone directed at his eyes, a brick for his head and a large stick for his back, all scored full marks. Then two of the rioters tried to pull him from his horse. Unable to do this, they mercilessly beat him on the base of his skull. But for the support of comrades who rushed to his assistance he would have crashed to the ground.

William Booth stood erect throughout the onslaught, encouraging his followers to go forward.

When the Salvationists reached the Albert Hall for the public gathering many of them were ' black as colliers, their bodies bruised and sore '. Uniforms were spoiled with blood and egg-yolk, and instruments were battered beyond use.

Their General looked at them with pride. ' *Now is the time to get your photographs taken,*' he exclaimed.

During 1882 nearly 700 officers and soldiers were brutally assaulted on British streets for proclaiming the gospel outdoors. They bore on their bodies the marks of the Lord Jesus.

Today, in many lands, the Army open-air meeting and march has become part of national life—a privilege bought at a great price.

Twenty-three

Why should the devil have all the best tunes?

THE theatre in Worcester was crowded for the visit of William Booth on January 22, 1882. Even the General himself ' had great difficulty in getting in '. The door was smashed by the crowd still trying to gain admission after the place was full.

George ' Sailor ' Fielder, the Commanding Officer, had been put up to sing. He had been a sea captain with a voice that had often been heard above the roar of the waves. (Forty years later he still had ' a voice like thunder and gloried in open-air fighting '.) He sang his testimony in the words, ' Bless His name, He set me free.'

' That was a fine song. What tune was that? ' inquired the Army's Founder later.

' Oh,' came the reply in a rather disapproving tone, ' General, that's a dreadful tune. Don't you know what it is? That's " Champagne Charlie is my name ".'

' That's settled it,' William Booth decided as he turned to Bramwell. ' *Why should the devil have all the best tunes?* '

The adoption of such music was soon put to full use. On Saturday afternoon, May 13, 1882, the congregation at the opening of the Clapton Congress Hall joined heartily in the chorus of Gipsy Smith's solo, ' O the Blood of Jesus cleanses white as snow ' to the music of ' I traced her little footsteps in the snow '. There were no qualms of conscience. Many people gathered there knew none of the hymn tunes or gospel melodies used in the churches; the music hall had been their melody school.

An early pamphlet made the Army's position clear by saying that it ' considers all music sacred when used with holy purpose '.

For his Christmas message to *War Cry* readers of 1880 William Booth had already written: ' Secular music, do you say, belongs to the devil? Does it? Well, if it did I would plunder him for it, for he has no right to a single note of the whole seven. . . . Every note, and every strain, and every harmony is divine, and belongs to us. . . . So consecrate your voice and your instruments. Bring out your cornets and harps and organs and flutes and violins and pianos and drums, and everything else that can make melody. Offer them to God, and use them to make all the hearts about you merry before the Lord.'

Today, however, we have to take great care in the use of music originally written for other purposes. International laws of copyright forbid much that the Army was able to do in earlier times. Nevertheless, music is still one of God's most valuable gifts to mankind.

Twenty-four

From the tap-rooms

THE year 1883 was one of great progress. It was also in the middle of a time of most brutal persecution. New buildings were being opened almost every week, and were being filled with inquiring people.

How to officer all these new corps with suitable leaders raised a problem and people asked William Booth where he would find his preachers. ' *From the tap-rooms*,' he replied. He knew that converted drunkards were the most suited people to bring more of their kind into the Kingdom.

He also wanted leaders from wherever they would come, for his aim was to win for God people from all walks of life. He would train them, if they had the basic qualifications.

Later he wrote about the type of men and women they would need to be; the sort of cadet he ' wanted, very much wanted indeed '.

'Any who have the notion they ought to be officers, would like to be officers? Any who don't like their present job, their present home, who don't like what they have to do, or don't like having to do at all? No, a thousand times no! Let us have the quality, any amount of quality.'

As the General wrote he used David as an example. ' Let us have Davids,' he called. David wanted to show that Jehovah was the King of kings. David was after the war and not the wages; he went to battle in the name of the Lord.

' This is the way to go to war,' William Booth continued, ' the royal way, the conquering way, the invincible way, the old-fashioned way.'

At first no training arrangements were possible. For example, Henry Bullard, leaving his Leamington home in 1880, was told, ' Make your will, pack your box, kiss your girl, be ready in a week.' He was thrown straight into the fight.

Earlier still, in Christian Mission days, when Marianne Faulconbridge (' the Zulu Queen ') was ' called ' from Coventry, she inquired about the possibility of a period of training. ' You must be like the Irishman's gun—go off, loaded or not,' William Booth replied. But both Henry and Marianne had the necessary qualifications and they remained fighters to their dying day.

The importance of having a system of training people to be evangelists (later officers) had been seen as early as 1877. George Scott Railton wrote to Bramwell Booth in November: ' Could we not have a centre in London to which all hopeful young folk could be rallied and where they could be thoroughly looked through and trained? ' Where they could be helped in ' the development of spiritual and natural powers '?

That wish has been fulfilled not only for London but throughout the world. Nevertheless, to quote the Founder's own appeal of 1883, ' are there not . . . some holding back that presentation of themselves to fulfil the consecration vows they have so often uttered ? '

Twenty-five

Be a believer in the dark!

THE year 1884 had been one of great variety. It had seen the inauguration of the Women's Social Work; the *Band Journal* and *All the World* had made their first appearance. Officers had suffered imprisonment for preaching the gospel; there had been serious riots in Worthing; the Founder's daughter Eva had been arrested for holding a meeting on the triangle in Mare Street, Hackney.

On the bright side, Canon Liddon, while preaching in St Paul's Cathedral, had made favourable references to The Salvation Army.

For the first issue of *The War Cry* of 1885, William Booth provided an article entitled ' New Year's Advice '. He had in mind the trials and successes of the year which had just closed. ' I hope all we Salvationists are looking forward to, and praying for, the New Year,' he wrote, ' because it promises to afford us new opportunities of getting more of the gifts of the Holy Spirit in our own souls and spreading salvation more effectively, pulling more sinners out of the fire and advancing more extensively the Kingdom of God.'

His writing was in the form of a letter to his ' soldiers who . . . spend all their strength for the salvation of men ' in which he called for a new trust—a new confidence.

He pointed out that anybody can believe when the enemy runs and the music plays, but there are times ' when the storm rages . . . the world mocks and the newspapers sneer '. Therefore he urged: ' In 1885 *be a believer in the dark!* ' He wanted the incoming year to be ' memorable and glorious in the annals of the salvation story '.

And what a year it proved to be!—one of the most successful in the Army's history. Over 400 new corps were opened and the number of officers serving in lands outside the United Kingdom doubled to nearly 1,300.

William Booth's followers gathered 393,000 signatures petitioning Parliament in Britain to change legislation and raise the age of consent from 13 years to 16 years. As a result the Criminal Law Amendment Act became law in August.

This was followed by the sensational trial of Bramwell Booth, who was acquitted, and William Stead, who was sentenced to three months' imprisonment for technically breaking the new law Salvationists had helped to bring on to the statute-book.

During the many anxious moments of the Purity Agitation, and at a time when Catherine Booth's health was causing greater and greater concern, the General could have sung meaningful words·which his people of today could well take as a motto:

> When we cannot see our way,
> Let us trust and still obey.

Twenty-six

Let us try a Self-Denial Week

' Look, Bramwell,' exclaimed William Booth to his son one morning in 1886, ' this officer's offer of his pudding money has given me a good idea. . . . It has occurred to me that all our people would be willing to deny themselves for one week of something in the way of food. . . . *Let us try a Self-Denial Week.*'

The day before, the Exeter Hall, London, had been packed with people keen to hear the General's plans for further extensions. Army work had not yet been commenced in Italy, Denmark, the Netherlands, Jamaica and Norway. Social work in Britain was in its infancy.

Preparations were in hand for forward movement, but money was short.

In that meeting William Booth's helpers moved among the congregation with small slips of yellow paper. 'Canaries' they were called, and Salvationists and friends alike were asked to write on them a promise stating the amount they were willing to give to help finance the new schemes.

One officer, Major John Carleton, who had already disposed of a business in Northern Ireland and had given his gold watch, had nothing more to donate.

But he passed in a 'canary': 'By going without my pudding every day for a year, I calculate I shall save 50 shillings.'

'I do not think any of my officers ought to go without their pudding for a whole year,' said William Booth when he read the promise to the congregation. 'They need all the food they can get, and probably more. . . . Men are more to us than money.'

No more Christlike method of helping the Salvation of our poor World was ever invented than Self Denial Week.

This years effort must go beyond all that have gone before it. You will do your part. Wont You?

William Booth.

A friend immediately posted two pounds, ten shillings to Headquarters to save the Major his sacrifice. The opening of that letter the next morning inspired Self-Denial Week, about which the General later wrote: ' No more Christlike method of helping the salvation of our poor world was ever invented.'

The first target of £5,000 was almost reached. People of all walks of life helped. Some city business men travelled in third- instead of first-class coaches for a week; many smokers gave up tobacco; children ran errands; William Booth himself took an even more frugal diet. The profits all went into the Self-Denial Fund.

And Carleton? What did he do? Many years later he was forced to admit that, despite the Army friend's gift to release him from his promise, he went without his pudding for a whole year!

Twenty-seven

Go and do something!

WILLIAM BOOTH was pacing the room but partly dressed and his hair uncombed, when his son Bramwell came in to make his customary early-morning call.

No calm word of welcome that morning was offered to the Army's Chief of the Staff.

It was December 1, 1887, and late the night before the Founder had returned from opening a new corps hall at Whitstable, Kent. Crossing London Bridge in a cab he had seen men lying and trying to sleep on the flagstones.

' Here, Bramwell,' he called. ' Did you know that men slept out all night on the bridges? '

When Bramwell Booth replied that he did, his father continued showing even greater concern: ' You knew that, and you haven't done anything? '

Valid reasons for not having been able to help the unfortunate men without a home were quickly forthcoming. Demands had been many for extensions to work already in operation; workers were few. Money was not easy to come by. The Army could not do everything.

' I don't care about that stuff,' came the rebuke from one who really loved the needy despite seeming inability to help to any worth-while degree. ' I've heard it before. *Go and do something!* Bramwell, do something! '

After more pacing and spoken wrath on civic authorities who allowed such a state of affairs, he continued: ' Get hold of a warehouse and warm it and find something to cover the poor fellows. Anything will be better than nothing! But mind, Bramwell, no coddling! '

The instructions were quickly followed and seven weeks later *The War Cry* contained the following announcement: ' To help these poor hungry, helpless crowds for this world and the next has long been our earnest desire. . . . We have now decided to do something toward alleviating this dreadful misery and have taken premises in the West India Dock Road, Limehouse, in which we propose to furnish a sleeping shelter for the night.'

That was but part of the plan triggered off by the sight of men on the bridge at night.

William Booth was not only a theorist; he was a doer. In turn he wanted no idle soldiers; he wanted workers. And he wanted to see initiative.

Once when he had discovered that some of his old clothes had been given away by his son to some needy fellows in the shelter he warned ' in his whimsical tone, and not without a note of reproof ': ' Bramwell, I wish you would do your charities at your own expense! '

Twenty-eight

The Cab Horse's charter

WHEN William Booth began his work in East London in 1865, the poor were very poor.

By 1890 he was more than ever disturbed by their needs. He would undoubtedly have endorsed the words spoken later, in 1965, by General Frederick Coutts before Her Majesty Queen Elizabeth II:

' If we ourselves, for want of a better way of speaking, refer to our evangelical work and also to our social work, it is not that these are two distinct entities which could operate the one without the other. They are but two activities of the one and the same salvation which is concerned with the total redemption of man. . . . Both have the same end in mind.'

Therefore, in 1890, Booth the preacher, the evangelist, began to be known also as a social reformer.

In October he published his book, *In Darkest England and the Way Out*. Twelve months later over a quarter of a million copies had been published, and the profits were ploughed back into the scheme outlined in the book.

He offered a plan, ' a very humble one, but if realized it would solve the worst problems of modern society '. He called it *The Cab Horse's Charter*.

He maintained that if a cab horse, the forerunner of the engine of a taxi, fell, we would do all we could to put it on its feet again, without any questions being asked. It had ' a shelter for the night, food for its stomach and work allotted to it by which it can earn its corn '.

' That,' he continued, ' although a humble standard, is at present absolutely unattainable by millions—literally by millions—of our fellow men and women.'

He described these needy people as ' the submerged tenth '. They were his people. He gave shelter to as many as possible. He opened a match-making factory, giving men and women honest work to do; and by using only

Salvation Army matches

safety matches he also helped to stamp out necrosis (phossy-jaw). He trained hundreds in agriculture at the Hadleigh Farm Colony and then sent them qualified to work overseas.

He and his followers have always kept the Cab Horse's Charter as the lowest standard. Today he would find some problems still unsolved. But nearly half the men who live in hostels in Britain sleep under an Army roof. He would have been proud of the world total of 150 industrial homes and occupational centres and the Army's 13 training farms.

Twenty-nine

Sing it again, Lawley!

WHENEVER William Booth preached he developed his thoughts toward the moment when he would appeal to his listeners to make a decision to serve Christ—on the spot.

He would call them to come forward and kneel at the Penitent-form and then launch into a prayer meeting.

In his earlier days he led this part of the meeting himself, but by 1890 he was beginning to feel the strain of taking full charge of protracted gatherings and needed help.

He was conducting a campaign in Durham. Assistance was essential, so he ' wired ' Colonel John Lawley to come at once. Lawley, later a Commissioner, was the man who interviewed candidates for officership. He could sing; he had outstanding earnestness. Surely he would be the ideal leader of the General's prayer meetings!

Lawley passed the test, and for twenty-two years the two men worked together. The Commissioner would carefully select the choruses to be used and make sure that the tunes were also helpful. On some tours he would have to choose suitable prayer choruses in five languages.

In prayer meetings William Booth would pray—and watch—as Lawley appealed to sinners to seek the Saviour. The Spirit of God would be at work upon the congregation; a man would move toward the front. ' *Sing it again, Lawley!* ' the General would call.

William Booth was never happy unless there were seekers in his prayer meetings. But sometimes he was disappointed.

' It was the queerest day I have had for many a year,' he wrote in an unpublished letter to his son Bramwell from one of his motor tours. According to the *War Cry* report, he had been ' received with all the paraphernalia of officialdom, surrounded by a big crowd of people '. He had accepted ' enthusiastic greeting ', had replied ' in choice and feeling terms ', and then ' hied to his billet '.

Although nearly 1,700 people attended one of his meetings, his own comment was: ' We had a very disappointing time . . . we did not get a single soul out, although a good many remained and there was much conviction.'

He had preached, he said, what he thought to be ' an extremely powerful sermon ', but what really mattered to him was missing—no one had knelt at the Penitent-form.

Thirty

Shout ' Hallelujah '

BERLIN police were on special duty, for British-born William Booth was announced to speak at the Athenaeum and the young *Heilsarmee* was still suffering from Prussian prejudice. A small crowd of Salvationists assembled at the front door as the Army's Founder stepped from his cab.

' Hallelujah! ' shouted one boisterous member of the welcoming party. ' Silence! ' cried Commissioner George Railton, who was responsible for organization and was fearful of his guest's safety. He felt that any unnecessary display of enthusiasm might give the police a pretext to close the meeting.

' What? ' retorted General Booth, ' stop a meeting for a Berliner praising God? . . . *Let the Salvationists shout " Hallelujah " wherever they are and whatever be the consequences.*'

The instruction ' wherever they are ' has been implicitly obeyed. When Salvationists from 70 lands gathered in London in July 1965 for the Centenary Celebrations, many were tied to their mother tongue. The only expression they had in common was ' Hallelujah! ' An Indian knew its meaning as he greeted a Brazilian and in the same way a Korean hailed an Italian.

The Japanese had been familiar with this international word for many years. As William Booth entered Yokohama Harbour in April 1907 he was welcomed by ' a distinctly original and enterprising salute in the form of daylight fireworks, let off from a launch '. The central feature was a group of exploding rockets forming the word ' Hallelujah ' in Japanese characters.

As early as March 1878 ' Hallelujah Lasses ' were appointed to the Christian Mission station at Felling-on-Tyne and five months before that, Elijah Cadman had called upon the people of Whitby to ' join the Hallelujah Army '.

' Whatever be the consequences,' said William Booth.

As mud and fireworks showered through the windows of the wool shed in Bethnal Green in 1869 his followers shouted ' Hallelujah '; and the same word rent the air of the court-house at Boudrey, Switzerland, when in 1883 William's daughter, Catherine, was acquitted after suffering 12 days' imprisonment in Neuchâtel prison for holding public meetings.

And let the cry still ring—' Hallelujah!'

Thirty-one

I come along with my drums and my trumpets

SHORTLY after his return from evangelistic campaigns in South Africa, Australia, New Zealand, India and Ceylon in 1891–92, William Booth was interviewed in his home at Hadley Wood by Raymond Blathwayt, who reserved his time for the princes of the pulpit, poets and authors.

The General spoke of the persecution of Salvationists in Eastbourne, of the welcome home he had received when nearly 7,000 of his soldiers had passed a saluting base at Marble Arch, London, and of the fact that ' publicity in all such cases means success '.

When the interviewer suggested that some of the Army's methods ' sometimes to the uninitiated perilously approach the blasphemous ', Booth looked solemnly and quizzically into his questioner's face and asked: ' Don't you think that the *dilettante* intonation . . . has failed as yet to touch the heart of the great seething masses surging around us? " The dearly beloved brethren " don't respond as they are expected to respond. Now, *I come along with my drums and my trumpets* . . . and at once I get a large and increasing following.'

Marching along the Ratcliff Highway, London,
in 1882

As he spoke, the General marched around the room ' beating an imaginary drum and blowing an unseen trumpet '.

He had always loved music. In a love-letter to Catherine 40 years before, he had written, ' Cling to the music.

Music, oh, it will move me to almost anything', and Harold Begbie claimed that ' William Booth was never so happy as when he was singing, and it was one of his greatest joys in life that all his children were musical, some of them among the first composers of Salvation Army music '.

A ' musical service ' was part of his programme for the War Congress in August 1878. He had expected more instruments, but was pleased with the example set by ' fiddlers and concertinists and clarion sounders ', one of whom would probably have been George Leedham, of Hammersmith, the first man to play a cornet in a Salvation Army meeting.

Within a few months, the Fry family of Salisbury formed a brass quartet and attended the open-air meetings to help the Captain to overpower the raucous singing of the opposing mob. William Booth was soon using the Fry's band in his meetings throughout the country.

By December 1879, a similar quartet went ' Christmas playing ' in Consett and became the first *corps* band.

In the spring of 1880 the General appealed in the columns of *The War Cry* for Salvationists to learn to play. Any spare instruments could be sent to headquarters—violins, bass viols, concertinas, cornets or any brass instruments, drums ' or anything else that would make a pleasant sound for the Lord '.

It was soon discovered that brass and drums were the most serviceable for outdoor work, for general accompaniment purposes and for attracting the people—and in most lands that has remained the order of the day.

Thirty-two

Time for a little prayer

A FEW moments after entraining at Paddington (London) for the West Country, William Booth noticed a particularly attractive young woman sitting in the same compartment. When he saw the book she was reading, thereby discovering that they had certain interests in common, he politely opened up conversation.

She knew of the work of the Army and admired the General's methods. She rejoiced in his successes, but wondered why some village corps, in places which she named, were unable to establish themselves. Was it because the people there tried to pray in extempore fashion? Would it not have been better to have taught them a number of prayers couched in beautifully prepared theological terms?

The Army's Founder—'Prophet of the Poor'— described the lack of education, the poverty, the struggles of many of his people. They prayed in the only way they knew. His listener accepted his explanation and her admiration increased. What a wonderful officer she would make, he thought, if only she would join his ranks!

Swindon Junction was but a few miles along the line and soon she would have to change trains. William Booth fell to his knees and quietly said: ' My secretary here will assist you with your baggage. *There is time for a little prayer.*' He then prayed fervently that an abundance of God's grace would be her portion.

' What a charming old man is your General!' she exclaimed as the secretary handed her rug into the compartment of another train.

The unexpected travelling companion was Miss Margot Tennant, soon to become Mrs Herbert Asquith, wife of Britain's Prime Minister.

The Army's Founder always believed in prayer. As 'Evangelist' of the East London Christian Revival Society (early name of The Christian Mission of 1866) he urged those who signed the membership card to '*pray* believingly, live holily, labour earnestly'. The advice printed on the card then continued: 'And success in winning souls is certain.'

Little wonder that on February 12, 1903, this man of God was invited to open the United States Senate with prayer!

Thirty-three

We want another Pentecost

As a song-writer, William Booth is best known for his ' O boundless salvation! deep ocean of love '. This, usually called ' The Founder's Song ', has been translated into many languages, and when an American officer visited Moscow in 1958 he was told that the singing of it was a popular feature of Baptist worship in Russia. Our present song book (1953) contains four more songs from the Founder's pen.

In 1894 the Army celebrated the 50th anniversary of William Booth's conversion. He made this an occasion for an appeal in *The War Cry* for a fund to enable greater extension of service to mankind.

To this he added his personal conviction: ' I stand just where I stood 50 years ago, proclaiming, through the same Jesus, full and free forgiveness for the worst and most hopeless of the sons of men and, through the same Holy Spirit, power to enable the weakest to master every evil in their own nature and to conquer every temptation.'

That was not enough! A month later, on April 14, he published in the same periodical ' another song by the

General to be sung at the jubilee campaigns in this and other countries '. He knew that his people must be spiritually fit for the great task on hand.

One of the lines of the song ran, ' *We want another Pentecost* '. He thought of the consuming power of the fire Elijah had called down on his Carmel sacrifice. He wanted divine fire, the fire of the Holy Spirit, one of the emblems of Pentecost, to fall on his 29-year-old Army. He knew that the power of his Army, and its continuance, would depend upon his followers receiving a personal experience of Pentecost.

Already he had proclaimed to officers met in council in Darlington: ' The baptism of the Holy Ghost means enthusiasm . . . that suffers, works, sacrifices, that no opposition can daunt and no enemies destroy.'

This was ever his theme, and when in 1906 he gave a New Year greeting to his people, he told them what he would do if he were called upon to live his life over again. At the end of his message he wrote: ' I should seek to be filled with the Spirit and aspire, like the apostles of old, to go about the world imparting the Holy Spirit, and breathing forth light and hope and power on the souls of men.'

If he were with us today he would still sing: ' We want another Pentecost, Send the fire! '

Thirty-four

An assembly of all our Commissioners

FOUR days before Christmas, 1896, William Booth visited Hawarden Castle, near Chester, to meet Mr William Ewart Gladstone, four times Prime Minister at Westminster, who was then retired from public life.

Friendly and stimulating conversation included a discussion of Booth's international Army, at that time working in over 30 countries; theology, to which subject Mr Gladstone had been giving special attention during recent years; and experimental religion, at which point the Army's leader described a Penitent-form scene he had witnessed only two days before at Keighley, Yorkshire.

' Now, excuse my asking,' Mr Gladstone inquired in a somewhat apologetic manner, ' but I am sure that the question of the successorship to the very important position you hold will have occupied your earnest attention. Will you tell me whether any arrangements have been made for filling up this post when the time arrives for your removal from it, and inform me, please, what that may be? '

When the 87-year-old politician learned that it was the General's duty to name his successor, he exclaimed: ' It is

Hawarden Castle

a peculiar position. . . . I think we must go back to the 16th century to find an example of a system of personal nomination by the person occupying the post of authority, similar to the one you have chosen.'

William Booth had already become anxious about the position and mentioned to Mr Gladstone a scheme which was being completed. This was, to quote the General's own report of the interview, ' for providing against the possible contingency of a General passing away who had neglected the appointment of his successor, or who, for some calamitous reason, had been proved incapable for, or unworthy of, his position, and for soliciting a new General in *an assembly of all our Commissioners* throughout the world '. The idea of the Army's High Council was coming to birth.

As far back as 1876 William had written to his son Bramwell: ' With my present feelings I should certainly name you to take my place in the event of my decease.'

Not until August 1890, when Catherine, dying of cancer, at last consented to ' occasional injections of morphia ', had the Founder legalized his intention to nominate Bramwell as his successor. Had he felt he could never continue without the support of his Catherine? However, his decision lay sealed in a blue linen-reinforced envelope for 22 years.

Eight years after the Hawarden visit, and resulting from Mr Gladstone's urgings, the 1904 Supplemental Deed of Constitution made provision for the calling of a High Council, a gathering first convened in 1929 and attended by 63 leaders including all Territorial Commanders and Officers Commanding, irrespective of their rank.

No longer has the General the responsibility of choosing his successor, and all gatherings of the High Council since the first have consisted of ' the Chief of the Staff, all the Commissioners and all the officers who during the whole of the two years prior to the qualifying date shall have

held the rank of full Colonel and shall at the qualifying
date be holding territorial commands in any part of the
world '.

Thirty-five

I am thinking

' GENERAL, what are you doing up at this hour? ' exclaimed
Bramwell Booth late one night as he called on his father,
who was still pacing his room. ' You should have been in
bed long ago! '

William Booth had a headache and was trying to find
comfort from a wet towel worn as a turban. He looked up
quickly and replied: ' *I am thinking. I am thinking about
the people's sins! What will the people do with their sins?* '

As the Army grew, the Founder's congregations
wanted to know about the work of his unusual Christian
body. Simple statements made by this world prophet and
social schemer became important. Government officials
took notice. But his never-dying aim was to persuade
men and women to give up their sins.

In 1898, William Booth was about to visit a town in the
east of England. The organizers did all that could be done.
They paraded the streets with a brass band, made
announcements wherever people stood about, delivered
circulars to every house . . . yet there was a weakness in
the arrangements.

The meeting had been timed for an hour when those
who needed to hear the message of the gospel were still at
work.

The General wrote to Bramwell, Chief of the Staff, in
no uncertain terms. ' When they did come,' he wrote,
' they found the place full of old Christian fogies and

plumed professors, who came out of curiosity and with whom Jesus Christ Himself could have done nothing.'

He then went on to vow that if he visited any more places like that someone else must go round in advance and arrange gatherings for the poor folk. ' If they say they cannot pay the expenses, cut them down and I will pay them out of my own pocket.'

To preach to Christians, who agreed with all he said and had already made and were keeping their commitments to Christ, was not his mission.

To ' go for souls, and go for the worst ' was his motto and his order to all who dared to be associated with him.

Thirty-six

Tears of the widows

To William Booth there was no such currency as dirty money. All gifts, whoever the donor, were gratefully received to help on his work of alleviating the sufferings of the needy. Sinners and saints alike were welcome to contribute to Army coffers.

He had a ready answer for his critics. On one occasion he accepted a donation from a man in high society, but one known for his agnosticism. Although some of his friends frowned on his action, the Army Founder's conscience was not uneasy. ' *We will wash it in the tears of the widows and orphans* ', he replied, ' *and lay it on the altar of humanity.*'

He never despised the shillings and pence of the poor; he included the smallest contributions in the subscription lists which contained recognition of help given by the wealthy.

Lord Rothschild appreciated William Booth's work and told him during an interview: ' I'm going to give you

£1,000, General.' Then in a teasing vein continued: 'When will you have it?' 'Now!' thundered the one-time pawnbroker's assistant as he thought of the hundreds of meals he would be able to provide for the hungry, or of the help it would be for some new building project. And the great financier reached for his cheque book.

Another time the Founder's son, Bramwell, was given a blank signed cheque. 'Fill it in and make it payable to the Army,' said the benefactor. He had seen William helping a costermonger loading scrap iron on to a wheelbarrow and had vowed, 'If that is the spirit of The Salvation Army, then I shall help it as I have opportunity.'

'Shall we say a thousand pounds?' asked Bramwell.

'Well—yes,' came the halting reply. 'As you have said *only* one thousand pounds, we will make it one thousand.'

One often wonders what the General said when he heard the story and realized what he could have done with five thousand!

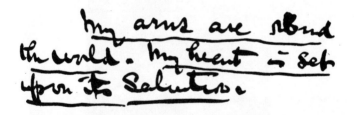

As an old man William Booth summed up his policy when he said: ' I have been trying all my life to stretch out my arms so as to reach with one hand the poor, and at the same time to keep the other in touch with the rich. But my arms are not long enough.'

Long enough or not, his arms stretched to their greatest span, relieving the poor and helping the rich to put their wealth to the greatest use.

Thirty-seven

I'd learn how!

' I SAW him walking backward in the dusk over an uneven wharf, his cloak blown upwards, tulip fashion, over his grey head while he beat a tambourine in the face of the singing, weeping, praying crowd who had come to see him off.'

This was Rudyard Kipling's description of his sight of William Booth just before the two men happened to embark on the same ship.

Kipling, young, still in his thirties, took the ' old man ' to task. ' Like the young ass I was,' he recalled years later, ' I expressed my distaste of his appearance at the wharf.'

The Fry family of Salisbury

'Young feller,' the warrior replied, 'if I thought I could win one more soul to the Lord by walking on my head and playing the tambourine with my toes, *I'd—I'd learn how!*'

The Army's Founder was always learning how. Sometimes his methods shocked more sedate Christians, but he was ever looking for ways of awakening sinners to their need of a Saviour and shaking the saints of his day out of their lethargy. One example must suffice.

Today we cannot think of an Army without bands. In April 1879 William Booth appointed Marianne Faulconbridge to the command of the Salisbury Corps. A few months earlier the Fry family had begun to use their instruments in the Army's meetings. They helped with the singing.

Poor Marianne was alarmed with the appointment. 'Mr Booth!' she exclaimed in dismay. 'A brass band! I don't think I should like it in connection with religious services!'

But William Booth had *learned* how to use a brass band in this manner and Marianne soon *learned* how to appreciate the musicians' help.

In the 1930s on the sands at Weston-super-Mare, Marianne (then Mrs Staff-Captain Pawson) was never happier than when a full band supported the singing of the holiday-makers.

Thirty-eight

Words that Mary Ann will understand

WHENEVER possible during his campaigns, William Booth would call his host and the household together before he moved on to another town. He would pray God's blessing on those who had entertained him and was never satisfied until the servants had joined the group.

When counselling his officers on the art of public speaking, he would say: ' *Use words that Mary Ann will understand*, and you will be sure to make yourself plain to her mistress; whereas if you speak only to her mistress, you will very likely miss her, and Mary Ann as well.'

' Clear, direct, vigorous, simple ' was the way Bramwell Booth described his father's vocabulary. He expected his helpers to follow his example.

Alex. M. Nicol, Booth's travelling companion on many a world tour, recalled how the Founder would hold morning prayers with his staff. In turn each would read the appointed Bible portion, the General adding his own spontaneous comments.

On one occasion, when the reading had been an incident from the life of Moses, William Booth remarked on the prophet's ability to train a group of slaves. ' Where did Moses get his political economy and statesmanship from? The land, the land, the land! And there is more common sense to be picked up on a farm than at Oxford or Cambridge. Let us pray! Cox, lead. And be short, and don't use big words.'

As early as 1867, a reporter was sent to the Effingham Theatre to secure copy for an article describing William Booth's meetings with an East End congregation. The writer found the building to be ' one of the dingiest and gloomiest places of amusement . . . perhaps in all London '.

But he continued:

' Mr Booth employed very simple language in his comments . . . frequently repeating the same sentence several times as if he was afraid his hearers would forget. . . . Not a word was uttered by him that could be misconstrued; not a doctrine was propounded that was beyond the comprehension of those to whom it was addressed. There was no sign of impatience during the sermon.'

Thirty-nine

I like my tea . . . hot

' Now, General, make yourself quite at home. We have everything here, and I have engaged a special chef from Paris to cook your food. Now, what will you have to begin with ? '

The speaker was a millionaire who had requested that he should entertain William Booth when he visited the town on one of his continental tours.

The General was tired after an important meeting, and on arrival at the mansion had been introduced to all the gathered celebrities before being asked to take his place at table.

In answer to the question, he politely apologized and explained that he was ' rather a tiresome eater ', taking ' very little for supper '.

Further pressed to take some light soup, or salmon, or even a drink of ' the best vintage from France ', he replied, ' No, thank you, sir. If you please, just a small basin of bread and milk! '

Embarrassments of this nature had been known before —but never again. From then on, a prospective host was given a menu of what William Booth could eat.

All his life he suffered from dyspepsia and world travelling must have been a real trial. As early as 1867 Miss Jane Short, who lived with and served the Booth family for five years, noticed how dreadful it was ' to see how the poor man suffered '. Over 40 years later she remembered that, despite this constant inconvenience, ' he would fling it all off directly there was work to do, or if he had to comfort anybody else, particularly Mrs Booth '.

In one of the last letters he wrote to his ' dear Eva ', on July 20, 1912, he referred to ' a return of my indigestion in its most terrible form '. No wonder, then, that a special diet was so essential!

To a letter sent on September 14, 1910, to friends in Dewsbury, who were preparing to entertain the 81-year-old warrior, was attached a detailed menu. The General could ' not take fish, flesh or fowl in any form '. Toast, butter, cream cheese, asparagus, potatoes or mushrooms ' as may be convenient ' and ' sometimes a little honey ' were the main items.

A significant paragraph reads, ' Before leaving for the afternoon meeting the General likes a cup of tea '; and if the tea was not really hot he would turn to the maid and whisper: ' *I like my tea as I like my religion—hot, very hot.*'

William Booth had no place for lukewarmness. No half-measures would ever satisfy this enthusiast. Even when he saw an officer ' doing well ' he would compliment him, then, almost in the same breath, remind him that ' this and better will do '. With him it was always, ' God shall have all there is of William Booth '; and nothing less should be the standard of those who in the second Army century are continuing his work.

Forty

My ambition is the souls of men

WILLIAM BOOTH was busier than ever. He was on the eve of the 15-day International Congress of 1904, which was to be attended by crowds filling the Royal Albert and Exeter Halls, and the Crystal Palace. The focal point was to be the International Congress Hall, specially erected in the Strand to seat 5,000 people.

He had made a last-minute inspection of this new hall, for he wanted it to be spic and span, a standard of cleanliness and order for visitors to London to see and copy.

He had an important engagement within the hour: 'the Rev. William Booth, Commander in Chief of The Salvation Army', had been invited to Buckingham Palace to meet King Edward VII that day, June 24.

There was no time to stand on ceremony just then. The hansom cab was outside; Commissioner George Pollard, who would accompany him, was waiting. Placing his top hat on a chair and bending down, the General washed his hands in a workman's bucket. He was then ready to visit the head of the British Empire.

Preparing to meet the King

The interview 'was of a most gracious and cordial nature'. The General was delighted to be able to speak of the work of his people in 49 countries. The King complimented him and asked how the churches viewed his work. 'Sir,' replied the 75-year-old warrior 'they imitate me.'

The King was amused and requested him to write in his autograph album.

> Some men's ambition is art.
> Some men's ambition is fame.
> Some men's ambition is gold.
> *My ambition is the souls of men.*

In those words William Booth summed up his life's work.

Of his many existing autographs another has a similar ring. When Colonel John Roberts, the first editor of *The Little Soldier* (later *The Young Soldier*), was a young officer, the Founder visited him and left this message: ' William Booth, General of The .Salvation Army, whose highest ambition is to be made equal by the Holy Ghost to the great opportunity opened before him by the providence of God.'

Forty-one

I have looked into the empty sepulchre

IN a burst of sunshine William Booth sailed from Marseilles for a short tour of the Holy Land. His visit to Jerusalem was to be *en route* to New Zealand, but to walk where Jesus had walked would be the fulfilment of a life-long ambition.

The Army's Founder arrived in Jerusalem on March 9, 1905. The journey had been trying; his health had been indifferent; and even the berth on the ship had been changed and had caused much inconvenience. But as the train chugged its three-thousand-foot climb from the sea to the place where Jerusalem's walls and towers came into view, his problems faded away; his mind was on preaching

Christ the Saviour of the world in the city of the Resur-
rection.

He visited the Pool of Siloam and a traditional site of
Calvary; he heard the beggars' plaintive wail of ' Back-
sheesh '; he walked in the Temple area and looked toward
Olivet.

In David Street a dark-skinned boy, wearing no more
than a small brown coat, ran toward him. The lad
dropped to his knees, touched the Englishman's boot with
his hand, then kissed his own little black fingers. Twenty
times he repeated this sign of affection for a godly man.

William Booth was unable to speak to him, but a smile
conveyed a loving greeting.

In Gethsemane he threw himself beneath the olive
trees; for were they not probably descendants of those
under which our Lord Himself prayed? Here Christ's

*William Booth wearing a sun helmet in the
Temple area, Jerusalem*

follower called upon God to bless the world. Seeing him
weary in the heat, a Carmelite monk offered welcome
refreshment, and the two men shared fellowship.

From Jerusalem the General issued a manifesto in

which he called his soldiers to a greater ' united, desperate, persistent effort to save the lost '.

He had been inspired, for he also wrote with triumph: ' *I have looked into the empty sepulchre.*' Empty! He served a risen Saviour. He knew the joys of Easter.

Despite his son Bramwell's warning, ' You will admit that you have rather a leaning to doing too much in the way of meetings', he led a number of gatherings which included a salvation meeting each evening. Twenty-two people knelt at the Penitent-form.

His main intention was to ' open fire ' in Jerusalem. He wrote to London clearly stating his wishes and less than three months later, even before he had reached home again, an officer was on his way.

No Army work was established, but Christians had caught something of William Booth's fire, and he himself had been filled with the unique wonder that comes to all sincere pilgrims to the cradle of Christianity.

Forty-two

Paint with a big brush

A THEATRE in Folkestone was crowded one summer day in 1905. William Booth had recently returned from a 30,000-mile voyage. He had visited the Holy Land, Australia and New Zealand. To a London newspaper reporter he appeared ' no more tired than a tidal wave ' and as having ' caught something of the sea's freshness and majesty '.

The 76-year-old warrior rose to address the holiday-makers who formed the first congregation of this, his second motor tour. It was to lead him as far north as Glasgow.

He spoke of the Army's work in all its branches. His listeners were moved as he told them stories of men in the antipodes who had been rescued from the lowest depths of society.

Many of the people William Booth yearned to lead to Christ were considered in some circles to be outside God's mercy.

'Ah,' he cried with hope of one who believed in salvation for the whosoever, ' to reach and gather these I must make a big sound, and *paint with a big brush*—big as the stars.'

No small strokes would do for the Army's Founder. He was never satisfied. For himself, and for his followers, it was ' this and better will do '.

Salvationists in 1905 were at work in 50 lands, using 30 different languages.

Twenty years earlier he had roared at a London rally, as he thought of the size of the world and urged his officers and soldiers to win the world for God: ' We must grow till our arms get right round about it! '

These words were quoted by Archbishop Donald Coggan during his enthronement address in Canterbury Cathedral on January 8, 1975, as he made a dramatic appeal for Christian unity. A reporter in the Cathedral felt he was standing on the launching-pad of a new evangelistic era.

The Army's arms are still growing; the yellow, red and blue paint is still spreading. During the past decade Taiwan, Malawi, Spain, Lesotho, Portugal and Venezuela have been added to the list and Army relief in time of need has been gratefully received in Bangladesh and Nicaragua.

William Booth would have been thrilled to hear Her Majesty Queen Elizabeth II say at Aberfan after the 1966 disaster: ' We have begun to expect The Salvation Army to be quickly on the scene with helpful service in any emergency.'

Forty-three

I think you are convicted

' COME and see me alone in my room,' said 33-year-old Winston Churchill, President of the Board of Trade, to William Booth one day in 1908 as they met on the stairs leading to the terrace of the Houses of Parliament.

There had been a little bantering when Churchill overheard the Army's General jokingly say that he would not like to meet him ' except in a room with seconds and a brace of pistols '.

William Booth recognized in this young cabinet minister a man of power and one who could help him in his schemes to ease the burdens of the poor.

In its series, ' Friends of the Army ', *All the World* (1908) included the future Prime Minister: ' There is freshness and breeziness about the personality of Mr Winston Churchill, whose sparkling conversation and stirring speeches have the ring of the reveille about them.'

Already, in 1906, they had discussed the General's plans for an Army colony in Rhodesia. The interview was recorded as having been ' very friendly ', but two years later the matter was still only a dream.

Another two years passed. The Rhodesia scheme had not materialized but William Booth wanted to do something permanent to help residents in Britain's prisons. Churchill was now Home Secretary and the General remembered the earlier invitation to visit him. An appointment was made.

The conversation lasted an hour and a quarter—' one of the most interesting interviews of my life,' William Booth recorded in his diary.

At the conclusion Churchill asked with a smile: 'Am I converted? ' Much had been discussed, both spiritual and material, during those 75 minutes, and the 81-year-

old General replied: ' No, I am afraid you are not converted, but *I think you are convicted*.' Even in matters of
business William Booth's words had a spiritual overtone.

Fifty-two years afterwards, when Winston Churchill
was in the Middlesex Hospital with a broken thigh, Regent
Hall Band played to him during its Sunday morning street
ministry. ' I am most grateful to you all,' read the
telegram received by Bandmaster Eric Rapp.

No doubt memories of that 1910 meeting were in Sir
Winston's mind.

Forty-four

I am going into dry-dock for repairs

SEVEN THOUSAND people filled the Royal Albert Hall,
London, on May 9, 1912, to listen to William Booth for
what proved to be the last time. There were no amplifiers
then in this great auditorium, but the crowd heard him and
remembered his words.

In Newport, Mon. (now Gwent), in 1909, he had been
compelled to cut short a motor tour because of trouble
in his eyes. Following an operation, he lost one eye. He
said he was like ' some old vessel that had run on to some
rocks and was being dashed to pieces by the storming
waves '.

But he had continued his work. He had made another
motor tour in Britain, taken a renewed interest in the
needs of prisoners, visited them in their jails, travelled
again in Europe from Italy to Scandinavia.

In January (1912) he had fallen down the stairs of his
home, but in February was in Europe yet again.

In the Royal Albert Hall he stood like a warrior. His
address was a series of reflections. He spoke of the things
he might have done with his life, the national roles he

might have played. Then after each suggestion he clearly showed how his Salvation Army had helped, and still was helping, to solve problem after problem.

Last public appearance

As though suddenly remembering the personal problem of eye surgery which he had to face again a fortnight later, he broke from his usual style of oratory.

'And now, comrades and friends,' he said as his words reverberated with the strange echoes of the hall, ' I must say good-bye. *I am going into dry-dock for repairs*, but the Army will not be allowed to suffer. . . . The Army will . . . by its marvellous success show to the world that it is the work of God and that the General has been His servant.'

Then the warrior spirit returned with a fresh burst. ' While women weep, as they do now, I'll fight. . . . While there is a drunkard left, while there is a poor lost girl upon the streets, while there remains one dark soul without the light of God, I'll fight—I'll fight to the very end! '

Colonel John Lawley, faithful attendant and helper, took the General's arm to lead him from the platform, but was stopped as William Booth looked toward the congregation. ' I'm not satisfied,' he said. ' I want to see the Penitent-form! '

Even when, a few days after the unsuccessful operation, he was told that he would never see again, he touched Bramwell's hand and said: ' I have done what I could for God and for the people with my eyes; now I shall do what I can for God and for the people without my eyes.'

Forty-five

The promises of God are sure

ON August 20, 1912, William Booth ' laid down his sword '. All his life he had been a fighter.

During his last weeks on earth, although he was blind and physically weak, he was still concerned with the priorities which had controlled his thinking and work since his boyhood beginnings in God's service.

He had seen his Army expand beyond his wildest dreams. Now he wanted its arms to stretch even farther. He begged his son Bramwell to open fire in China as soon as possible. He pleaded that special care should be given to the homeless and to children.

When Bramwell Booth had listened attentively, his father pushed out his hand and asked, ' You promise? It's a bargain. Then give me your hand on it.'

' *You promise? It's a bargain* '

A few days before his promotion to Glory, the Founder was helped from his bed to a chair. His speech was failing. Bramwell, daughter Lucy and a nurse were giving close attention, ready to meet his every need.

' Bramwell—the promises,' he whispered. ' The promises.' Then someone prompted him by adding ' of God '. That was the thought in the old man's mind; and slowly, with great effort, he went on: ' *The promises—of God—are sure—are sure—if you will only believe.'* Almost every word was punctuated with a movement of the hand.

That immortal truth was William Booth's last statement to the world. He had always depended on God. He had proved that His promises never failed. And he knew that God expected him to remain true to all his promises.

The General had demanded much of his followers. The promises his officers had made to him often alarmed more mercenary-minded Christians, but he had never asked for more than he would give himself.

The making of promises is still in the Army constitution —even for young people. When they become junior soldiers they promise ' to pray, to read my Bible and, by His help, to lead a life that is clean in thought, word and deed '. And they can be sure—like William Booth—that God will be as good as His promise: ' I will be with thee: I will not fail thee, nor forsake thee.'